MW01148877

Black Biblical Coloring and Story Book 1:

History of Our Fathers

By: Moreh YAHUtsadeqnu James Darby IV

Beyt YAHUtsadeqnu Books 2013

(The House of YAHUtsadeqnu Books)

Copyright © 2013 YAHUtsadeqnu James Darby

IV (Beyt YAHUtsadeqnu Books)

All rights reserved

Book 1:

History of Our Fathers

About This Book (for the Parents): This book was written and illustrated in response to seeing years of historically inaccurate illustrations of biblical characters which in turn deeply impacts and destroys the self image of many black children whom themselves are the number one candidates for matching exactly the descriptions of the biblical Israelites. These falsely illustrated biblical books not only damage black children, but all children by making them believe a lie rather than the historically accurate truth. The Roman historian Tacitus on the Jews, in *The Histories*, Book V, c. 110 CE , said that in his day "Many, again, say that they were a race of Ethiopian origin " (he and his people, the Romans encountered Israelites during that time very frequently). A second Roman by the name of Emperor Justinian placed on Roman coins his own image, which was very obviously European in type on one side, and on the other he placed an image of a very arguably African type person in whom he recognized as the Hebrew Messiah YAHUshua'/Yeshua whom some call Christ Jesus. This is important to note because historically the only European/white type peoples in that area during that time were the Greeks and the Romans.

Note that ethnically, the Hebrews were neither Greek nor Roman but were often confused as being Egyptians earlier in their history by virtually all of their neighbors. Another purpose of this book is to repair and rebuild the self image of black children while giving all children a truthful and accurate view of what was happening in scripture so that they may have a deeper, more meaningful understanding, and appreciation for scripture. It is my prayer that this book is a great asset to whomever reads or colors it.

Why a black biblical coloring/story book (for the Parents): I simply call it a black biblical children's book so that the primary and target audiences can find it more easily but it is not simply a black biblical children's book but this and my following books are for all children. Instead, it is a historically accurate (as accurate as possible) biblical children's book representing the ancient biblical Israelites (The Hebrews) and others peoples with their proper and accurate physical features, characteristics, clothing, and landscape. Some may argue it doesn't need to be drawn with black people because color doesn't matter even if it is more historically accurate. If that were to be true then it still wouldn't matter that I have illustrated this book with their proper ethnic and physical traits because those who have illustrated the inaccurate pictures would not have originally considered race in their inaccurate illustrations and instead would have drawn the Israelites as a multiracial group sharing all peoples physical traits. Although, that in itself would be nonsense because if you are going tell the story about the truth you better tell it right and truthfully. Also to say that race for the bible doesn't matter is like saying you should not correct known mistakes after they have been made. Would you tell Chinese history and illustrate it with all blacks and sell that as historical truth believing that it is truthful and ok, very clearly no. Also, when you lie to children with false stories (like christmas and easter etc.) or you lie about these details it creates distrust between parents and children and makes it harder for children to find their parents believable or take them seriously later on in life vis a vis rebellion. I myself, as the author of this book, do not hold to a racial superiority doctrine. We are descendants of Noah and children of Adam and every people are great and beautiful in there own right for we are all made in the likeness and image of The Most High YHWH. We all have our ugly actions in history and we all share the common story of corruption from the garden and then onward to redemption and repentance back to our Creator YHWH. This book is to simply display truth to all people but primarily and specifically to restore those things of a lost heritage to it's forgotten people and their children.

Preface (for the Parents): In Book 1: "Stories of our Fathers", Great care has been taken in this book to make clothing, scenery, and people as historically accurate as possible just as the cover illustration of this book series was directly inspired by the Assyrian carvings of the Israelite captives of Lachish and the Egyptian inscriptions of what appear to be Hebrew Brick workers. The Assyrian carvings of the Israelite captives of Lachish may be the only historically verified carvings of the Ancient Israelites/Hebrews and I feel it is wonderful to note that these carvings are indisputably African in feature, displaying everything from wide noses and full lips, to coarse and knotted hair, Ethiopian style corn rolls, and even dreadlocks. The stories are recounted in very simple and plain English to make it easy for the children to understand with parents reading to them or if they read by themselves (depending upon the reading level of the child). The English names for all of the biblical characters have been used so to avoid unfamiliarity with the biblical characters whom people are more familiar with by English names (i.e. Elijah instead of EliYAHU). The English titles of God and Lord for the most part have been avoided because of their pagan roots and historical inaccuracy except when to explain the Hebrew term El (meaning deity) or shortened name YAH (the shortened/nick name of the deity of the Hebrews). The name of The Most High has only been used in its shortened form (YAH) simply because of discrepancies amongst certain groups surrounding its true pronunciation, as well as a great amount of unfamiliarity that most people have in regard to it. If any of these linguistic nuances are unfavorable when reading, feel free to replace words with the Hebrew or English terms you or comfortable with (i.e. Mosheh in the place of Moses). The colors used on the cover have been modeled within the range of Prussian Blue (tekhelet/takelet), Crimson, and Tyrian/Royal Purple which were the three colors that downed the curtains of the Temple in ancient Israel along with linen and gold. These colors can be seen as a sort of National colors of Ancient Israel if there were to be any.

Table of Contents

Adam and Eve

(Genesis Ch. 1-2)

cc91

Adam and Eve were the first people that The Most High created. After He made the sun, the moon, the earth, the stars, the land and the sea, the plants and the animals, He made Adam in His own image. He made Adam from the dust of the Earth on the sixth day of creation. Afterward, Adam saw that there was no one among the animals like him, so the Most High put him into a deep sleep and took one of his ribs. From Adam's rib He then created Eve so that he wouldn't be lonely. Adam and Eve are the father and mother of all people and they both rested on the Sabbath. Adam in Hebrew means "red" from the Hebrew word Adom/Adum and also earth from the Hebrew word Adamah (red earth kind of like clay). What color was Adam?

Noah's Ark (Genesis Ch. 6-8)

After Adam and Eve had many children, the Earth became filled with evil and sin. The whole earth became corrupted (dirty). There was only one man who was still good and clean on the whole Earth. So The Most High chose him and his family to restart the earth because The Most High was going to wash the Earth and cleanse it with a flood. This man's name was Noah. One Day, The Most High told Noah to gather two of every animal on the earth, one male and one female, and seven couples (fourteen total) of every clean animal which was seven males and seven females. The Most High then told Noah to build an Ark, which is a boat made for very strong storms and floods that water cannot get into. Noah built the ark and put all of animals in it. When The Most High sent the flood to wash the Earth, they were safe in the ark and stayed in it until all of the waters dried up.

After the flood, there was no one who had more faith in or a better relationship with The Most High than Abraham. Abraham was a friend to The Most High. They were such good friends that The Most High promised Abraham that he would bless his children to be a great nation. They would be so blessed that they would bless all other nations. He also promised to make them the greatest nation on earth. At the time that the Most High made this promise to Abraham, he did not have any children. Although Abraham was a very old man, Abraham believed that The Most High would still bless him and He did, with a son named Isaac. When Isaac got old enough, The Most High wanted to test Abraham to see if he still had faith and if he loved his son more than The Most High and so He asked Abraham to give Isaac back to him. Just as Abraham was going to give Isaac back ,The Most High sent an Angel to tell Abraham that he should give the ram caught in the thicket to The Most High instead, because it was only a test. This happened atop Mt. Moriah.

6

(Gen Ch. 32:24-28)

Jacob the son of Isaac the son of Abraham was the son of the promise. Jacob's twelve sons would go on to be the twelve tribes of Israel. They would become the greatest nation of all time. One day when Jacob was going to meet his brother Esau, he went to a place called Bethel (which means "House of The Most High"). There, he saw a Man sent by The Most High and Jacob wrestled him. Jacob told the man that he would not let him go until him go until he blessed Jacob. The man touched the hollow of Jacob's thigh and his hip popped out of socket. Then the man told Jacob that his name was no longer Jacob. His new name was Israel, because he won with both man and The Most High . In the picture, the hills of Mahanaim (Two Camps) and the shallow place where the river Jabok can be crossed, which is near Bethel, are both in the background.

Moses at the Burning Bush (Exodus Ch. 4:6-7)

The twelve tribes of Israel went to Egypt because there was a famine in their homeland. One day, a new ruler, or Pharaoh, rose up in Egypt. He was afraid of the Children of Israel (who were also called the Hebrews) so he made them slaves. Moses was one of the children of Israel but he was never a slave. Instead, Moses lived in Pharaoh's house until he had to runaway to Midian because he hurt an Egyptian for hurting a Hebrew man. One day in the land of Midian, where Mt. Horeb and Sinai* are, Moses saw something strange upon the mountain of Horeb. Moses saw a bush that was on fire but it didn't burn up. He went to the bush and he heard a messenger of the Most High speak to him and say, "Take off your shoes because the ground you stand on is set apart (very special or holy). Then the Most High spoke to Moses from the burning bush and told Moses that he was going to be chosen to lead his people out of Egypt to their own land and that they wouldn't be slaves anymore. Then The Most High would make them his people (Exodus ch 3). The Most High then showed Moses many miracles. One miracle was that, although Moses was dark skinned, The Most High made his hand as (leprous) white as snow and then made it return to its natural color . The Most High gave Moses the power to part the Red Sea and turn water into blood. Moses also made daytime look like night and called many animals against the Egyptians to free his people. Moses later wrote the first five books of the bible. In these books, he taught The Children of Israel proper laws from The Most High on how to behave as a nation, the true history of the world, and how to love and treat people the right way.

*Today Mt. Sinai and Mt Horeb are called Jebel El Lawz. Sinai is the mountain that is still burned today from the presence of The Most High resting upon it. (Exodus Ch 19:16-18)

Samson fighting the Lion (Judges Ch.14:5-6)

Long after Moses lead the children of Israel out of the land of Egypt to their own land Israel, the Children of Israel did not do the works of their father Abraham and they turned their backs on The Most High. When they turned their backs on Him, the evil nations who were around took control of the land and oppressed them. When this happened, The Most High always sent great men that were loyal to Him to save The Children of Israel out of their troubles to show them that He still loved His people. One of these men was Samson who had seven long locks of hair. He was a Nazarite from inside is mother's womb, which means he never cut his hair or drunk strong drinks like wine, which gave him a special connection to The Most High. Samson was so strong that he lifted an entire city gate and carried it on his back. Samson also defeated one thousand men with the jaw bone of a donkey. Samson also was fa-

mous for defeating a lion with is bare hands.

David vs. Goliath (1 Samuel Ch. 17)

David was the second King of Israel and one of greatest and most famous kings of all time. David really loved The Most High and had great faith that The Most High could do anything. David was a great musician and poet and wrote the Book of Psalms. David was also very wise and brave and mighty. When David was still a boy, there was a giant from the evil nations around them named Goliath who challenged the men of Israel, shouting that no one could defeat him. All the men of Israel were afraid of Goliath but David who was only a boy was not afraid of Goliath, David stood up to challenge Goliath and defeated him only with his faith in The Most High and a sling shot. Before defeating Goliath, David said to him, "You come to me with sword and spear and javelin but I come to you in the name of The Most High" (1 Samuel 17:41). Before that,

David was just a humble shepherd boy and the youngest of eight children, but he was able to defeat both a lion and a bear to save his sheep. David and Goliath are seen fighting in the valley of Elah (named after the terebinth or oak tree).

* 1 Samuel Ch. 17: 41 one is where the battle starts

Elijah, Elisha, and The Chariot of Fire

(2 Kings 2:11)

During the time that Ahab, the worst kings to ever rule Israel, was King of Israel, his wife Jezebel, who was one of the most evil women in history, was trying to kill off all of the men of The Most High. The Most High then sent the Prophet Elijah to punish them and stand up for The Most High and his people. Elijah did many miracles like calling fire from the sky, stopping the sky from raining, and parting the waters of the river Jordan. Elijah also brought a young boy who died back to life. Elijah had done many great things and proven that The Most High YAH is the only true El (El means is GOD in Hebrew and Elijah's name Eli-YAHU means "My El is YHWH"). After all of this Elijah was very tired. and so The Most High told Elijah that He would take Elijah to Heaven. Before Elijah could go to Heaven he had to teach someone to take his place. That persons name was Elisha and he was bald. One day they were walking together and Elijah told Elisha that it was the day that he must be taken to Heaven.

Elisha then asked for twice the spirit that Elijah had and that means to be twice as powerful. Elijah then told Elisha, "if you see me when I am taken up, then I will throw down my mantle to you and then you will have twice my spirit". They continued to walk and then all of a sudden a Chariot and Horses of Fire came and took Elijah into heaven. Elisha saw it happen and Elijah threw down the mantle, giving him twice the spirit of Elijah. Elijah was known for wearing a leather belt and being a hairy man.

Jonah and the Great Fish

(The book of Jonah)

Jonah, just like Elijah, was a prophet of The Most High. Prophets were The Most High's special spokesman, who could predict the future, and do any miracle The Most High told them to do, just like Moses. Jonah was chosen to warn the people of Nineveh near Babylon that if they didn't stop doing all the evil they were doing, that destruction was going to come upon them. Jonah didn't want to warn them because they were really evil people and he thought that they needed to be punished. The Most High still wanted to warn them because He is not happy watching people suffer and He wants everyone to have a chance to stop doing bad things. Jonah ran away and got onto to a ship because he really didn't want to warn them and thought that they should be punished. Later on, The Most High sent a storm that rocked the ship and Jonah was thrown into the sea. Then a very great fish, swallowed Jonah up. Jonah stayed in the belly of the fish for three days and three nights. Jonah began to sing to The

Most High and praise Him. Jonah realized that The Most High was right and good for what he did and for trying to warn the people. The Fish spat up Jonah on the shore and Jonah went to warn the people. When the people heard the warning, everyone in the city became afraid. Everyone from the King of Nineveh on the throne to the poorest person in the street all began to fast, repent (that means to stop doing evil), and to ask for forgiveness and mercy. They thought if they fasted and repented that The Most High would have mercy on them and save them from destruction. They were right, because He did have mercy and forgave them.

*Some people believe that the great fish may have been a whale because there is no real word specifically for whale in Hebrew. Also the whale is the only known animal big enough to swallow a man whole without harm. A whale also can evacuate the water swallowed from its mouth, leaving a pocket of air that can be recycled through its blow hole. This would be ideal for what Jonah experienced.

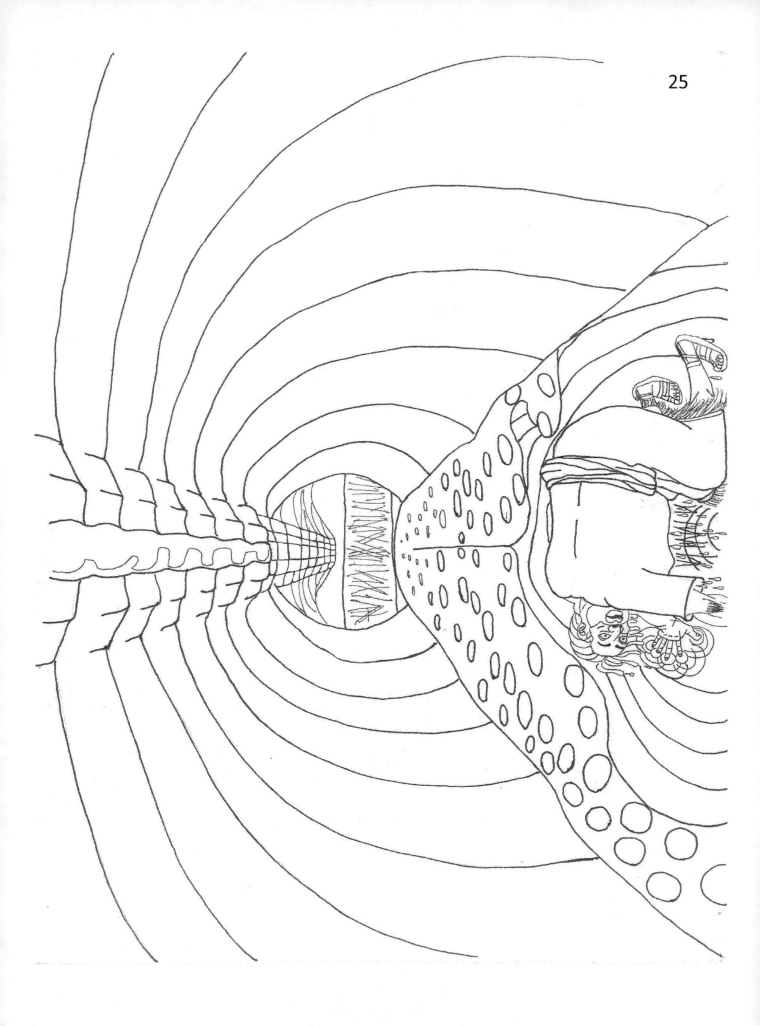

Daniel in the Lions Den

(Daniel Ch. 6)

After The Most High continued to save his people, the Children of Israel, and bless them and do many miracles for them they continued to turn their backs on Him and so He stopped fighting for them and then their enemies defeated them. They were then taken to Babylon for seventy years. Babylon was one of the most evil places in history, but The Most High still loved and blessed His people there. One of the Children of Israel in Babylon was Daniel. He was a very wise man who The Most High gave the gift to tell you what any dream meant. Daniel loved The Most High and was very faithful to Him and so The Most High made Daniel very wise and made him one of King Darius's wise men. Daniel would still pray and ask The Most High for forgiveness for himself and his people three times every day but the King's men in Babylon hated Daniel for being so wise. The King's men then tricked the king into making it illegal for anyone to pray to anyone or serve anyone who was not the king. Although, Daniel and King Darius were very good friends, Daniel was very loyal to The Most High and would never pray to anyone else. The punishment was that Daniel was to be thrown in the lion's den. The king became upset and did not want to do it, but he had to follow the royal laws. Daniel kept faith in The Most High and when morning came King Darius went to see if Daniel survived. Daniel was completely un-harmed and King Darius was amazed and praised The Most High because of it. King Darius was then angry at the men that tricked him, and threw them into the lions den. Afterward, King Darius told everyone in the kingdom to worship The Most High YAH, whom Daniel worshiped and served. On one of the rocks, the word "king" is written in ancient Persian, just as the scripture says that King Darius (who was a Mede and not a Hebrew) and his men sealed the entrance to the lions den with their sig-nets.

Acknowledgements: First, I would like to give thanks to The Most High for blessing me with the skills, the knowledge, the wisdom, and the understanding to produce this book. Next, I would like to thank my wife for her support, editing, and encouragement. Next, I would like to thank brothers YadaYAHU ben Yisra'el and Hondo Solomon for all of their support, encouragement, and help with publishing books. Finally, I would like to thank all of my friends and family who have supported or given encouragement like (don't worry I will not use full names) Uncle Taj, Albert, Papa James, ChazaqYAHU, Shaferah Haddasah, Tehillah, my Father and Father in Laws, my Mother and Mother in Laws, and siblings, Ashley Awani, Kazi, Jeremy, Cammeron, Joey, Jordan, and Mr. Eric as well as all else whom have given words of encouragement.

Coming Soon:

Book 2: Stories of our Mothers

Like Book 1 "History of our Fathers", Book 2 "Stories of our Mothers" covers several biblical stories except this time the stories of the women of the scripture are the focus. Another wonderful coloring and story book for parents and kids to spend time learning scripture and having fun.

Book 3: Animals of Israel connect the dots

This book has several different animals found commonly in ancient Israel as well as fun facts about the creatures and the biblical stories and scriptures that they are found in.

Book 4: Places in Israel

Book 4: "Places in Israel" is a great Coloring and Story book that displays many of the beautiful and stoic landscapes of Israel as well as scriptures of the legendary stories that happened in those places.

Book 5: Israelite Items

Book 5: Israelite items, details many of the common items of ancient Israel and associated scriptures from the Ark of the Covenant, to the 10 Words (10 Commandments), clothing, tools and more. Some pictures will be connect the dots and others for coloring.

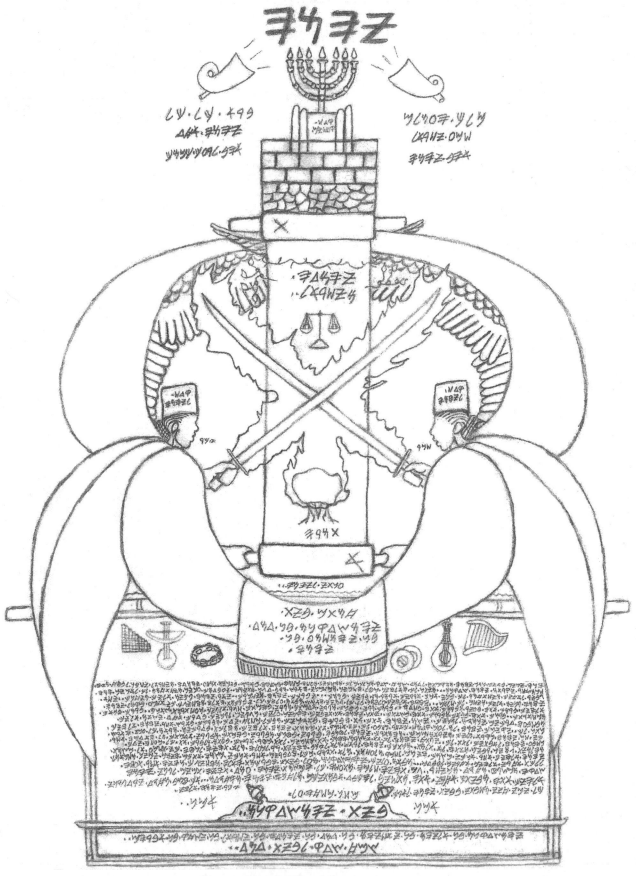

This is my family seal, "The Seal of the house of YAHUtsadeqnu". Look for this seal of approval on the back for more of my books. Page not for coloring

About the Author: (Moreh) YAHUtsadeqnu James Darby IV has previously taught scripture with the N.O.Y. (The Nation of Israel in Exile) and is currently working on producing several other works for adults and children. He is also an Artist, a Brick Mason, been a co host on several radio shows, and is currently studying to receive certification as a Master Herbalist and a Master Aromatherapist.

20962229R00025

Made in the USA
San Bernardino, CA
30 April 2015